GOD'S RED ROAD

THOMAS FENTON

Drawings by DAVID GRICE

Questions for the Road
p. 85

CARGATE PRESS
25 MARYLEBONE ROAD, LONDON N.W.1

PROLOGUE

It is easy to have the last word with God. He is satisfied with the last thought. There are many valid reasons why I should not be a missionary but I am sure they are not valid for Him. Before I accepted the call I astonished myself with the arguments I could furnish against it. But He left me with a thought—an afterthought. He always wins on afterthoughts. That is why I am now bending over this typewriter, why I am straining my eyes by this miserable lamplight to see what I have written.

That day we stood in the kitchen, Helen and I, talking about the situation in the Ivory Coast we knew we could not escape. Life would never have been the same if we had, for God's evidence is cumulative. His call brings with it all the half-forgotten vows credited to an over-worked emotion, all the half-opened doors of neglected crises and all the half-formed prayers, left jagged in the past lest He should really answer them. Without these, spiritual conviction would become a life-sentence of misery. Without them, Paul picking himself up off the Damascus Road, or Francis Thompson "clinging to the mane of every whistling wind," become pantomime acts; with them, they become, at least, madness with meaning. As I hung the teacloth on the line in the kitchen I knew there could be no dodging the issue.

A few weeks later the letter of acceptance arrived from the Missionary Society. I stood looking at the bold heading on the paper and I saw again those men I had tried to forget, those African sailors lined up on board the base ship in Freetown harbour while their gear was being searched below. I heard again the comments of the petty officer as he called them a pack of dirty good-for-nothing low-down thieving scum. I saw that look, which I now know so well, that look of sad patience on the faces of those men. How quickly the memory shuttles through time and weaves a nightmare of remorse or of broken intentions! There was that solitary black head in the ship's sickbay, so ominously still that I was reminded of black death. I remembered looking down at him through the ventilator in the deckhead and hearing the doctor say to the sick berth attendant: " He could get better if he wished but he is just willing away his life." I wondered what breed of men was this which could slip away from life as quietly as a boat drifts away on the tide. Perhaps I had to learn what life meant to these people to know why death is so often an advantage.

A little of its meaning became clear the day I went ashore and saw a youth with a withered leg. On his shin was a large green crater. He was stretched on a low verandah and a dirty cloth covered the wound. Twenty miles from Freetown by water was too far for a life to be saved. He died.

I remembered all this. I saw them there, those Africans, laughing, clowning, begging, cursing, being spoilt, being kicked about, ill-treated. And I said to myself: these also are God's flock—His own black sheep. But where are the shepherds? There was one shepherd and he, a missionary for seventeen years, had struggled in Christ's name to make a resurrection in the hearts of men, when reason

2

had judged it hopeless, for even the hot green hills borrow rain to simulate sorrow and mourn for the living dead heaped in the valley. It is a triumph of Grace that men are saved there but triumphant Grace will dominate the scene, when firmly set in human faith. Where, then, were the men to help that man? By what right had he been left without support? What right? My own right to leave him there. I remembered saying that if I came safely through the war I would go where Christ wanted me, even to Africa. Let Him show me the way clearly and I would go.

I folded the letter accepting me as a missionary. That was it. I knew what it would mean, for even if this is now no longer called the " White Man's Grave " one can still feel buried alive. But I am not fool enough to barter my life for a dream. Either I take reality with me or I waste my time. " None but Jesus can do helpless sinners good " even though they still go on being bad, and He was out there long before I heard of Africa. He, Who came to call sinners to repentance, must surely be there wading through the swamps, dragging His cross through the tangled bush, lying breathless by the roadside, staggering on to His modern Calvary until jeers die in the throat, until fetishers crush their little stocks of horn and feathers in hands made clean by the Son of Man, until the eery light of the forest is set at nought by the love of God shed abroad in the hearts of men. He is there already. The work of redemption is begun. What does it matter whether He wants me or not. I must follow.

This is the strange compulsion of His call, this is the bitter satisfaction of obedience, this is the glory of His service that here, even here, where so many victories are

3

crowned with defeat He is present to share it all. His presence ensures the end. If I fail, He cannot. This is the only relationship which can give my work significance. And, after all, why should I doubt my faith in Him? When a French Administrator took me in his gleaming Renault to see the plot of ground he had reserved for the Mission I did not expect to be driven a kilometre into the bush. But he told me that the centre of the new town would be on that very deserted piece of land. I build on the word of man; I cannot then hesitate over the promise of Christ. If, like the Administrator, Christ has only a red road to prove the work has begun, I shall believe it runs from Golgotha to the Ivory Coast.

If there is so little accomplished to justify my faith to the faithless, there is the everlasting love of Christ to sanctify it in His service. As I mark out the site for the Mission in a town which is yet to be, so I shall stake a claim for Christ in the Ivory Coast and with greater certainty, for He will achieve His glorious work and the eternal city will rise up out of the primordial bush.

I

WHEN Lepri returns from market with his *atieki* I shall leave for Bodou. My things are packed and stowed in the van. How many times have I set off like this! In the early days I kept a list of all the things needed and I would tick off each item as I put it in the box. That list is no longer necessary, but the boxes and their contents are the same. Even Lepri, who was a tiny fellow when I first came to the Ivory Coast, has not changed, except in stature. Now, as then, he asks permission to go to market just as we are setting off on a journey. When he returns in a few minutes he will wear the same good-natured grin, which will give place to a martyred air if I complain that he has kept me waiting.

How could he, Lepri, keep monsieur waiting? In any case, what is waiting? It is life. These Europeans run here and there shouting orders and urging people to hurry, but life without waiting would be meaningless. Every shop, office and railway station has its customers waiting patiently at the counter. Monsieur himself once waited fifteen days to buy stamps. The Chief had gone out for the day and had taken the key; the key had been left behind in the house; the clerk was too busy dealing with telegrams; they were out of stock of that particular denomination.

Newcomers to this country hold up their hands and cry: "What a country!" and talk feelingly of the value of dynamite. Others see that this tropical complacency has nuisance value and accuse the Africans of race prejudice.

The truth is that Africa is timeless and her children free of the burden of passing hours. Only now is there appearing that new class of men, those who take time seriously. They are the clerks and Government officials, who carry gold watches and live like Europeans. The common people call them " *petits blancs.*" For them, life has become the slow ticking over of precious minutes at the rate of so many francs for every completed sixty.

For the rest, the great majority, the people amongst whom I work, the day comes with the sun and the night brings the stars, the vibrating tom-tom, hot sticky dances, the taste of dirty sand and the smell of sweaty bodies, laughter, chatter, sleep. Months pass unheeded, years are of little moment. These are the people of the everlasting " Now," whose problems of yesterday are never pro-jected into to-morrow. How can there be " waiting " for these people when they have no defined idea of what is future?

So I wait here in the early morning. The sun's oblique

rays pick out the details of all created things more emphatically than the photographer's spotlight. I am compelled to notice once again the crimped texture of African hair, the tiny shadows on the uneven red bricks of the Girls' School wall, and the scars on the market woman's face as she shuffles by with her load of yams balanced on her head. Trickling perspiration looks wetter in this early morning sunlight, veins are bigger and more ominous, old cloths thrown hastily over the shoulders of old men look very old. Truth is abroad at this hour of the day, truth which is always waiting, truth, seen but not registered by these people, who pass the early morning picking their teeth with carefully chosen sticks cut from the Mission hedge. The sun comes up red. The sky changes colour. Every palm frond reflects a liquid gold, every grass roof is touched with morning magic. The African takes the stick from his mouth and spits.

With all the time to stop and stare they do not see what I see. But they see other things. It was during my first visit to Bodou that the leader of the Church told how one morning he noticed that a small patch of earth had been turned over close to the cross roads. He dug with his fingers until he touched the neck of a bottle. His suspicions thoroughly aroused, he ran back to the village and called out the people. Together they unearthed a bottle full of liquid and a small leather bag. The leader placed both in front of me.

" These things have been put in our path to do us harm, but we have found the man, and I should like you to see him."

He was a stranger. He had the long limbs and clean features of a North African.

" Did you plant these things at the cross roads ? " I asked.

" Yes," he replied, with a smile which revealed a row of even white teeth.

" Why ? "

" I am a foreigner, and, as the people have been good to me, I wanted to return their kindness, so I buried these charms to protect them from evil spirits."

" Do you want to be protected ? " I asked the people.

The leader answered for them all: " He is a liar. He thinks he can fool you, but he cannot fool us. He wants to do us harm."

These people see things. Their seeing has a practical value. They know when a clod of earth has been turned over, and, seeing, they want to know why. One day they will see a beautiful thing and they will ask the same question, and God himself will give the answer.

II

THERE are five roads out of Dabou, five red roads, five open wounds trickling through the forest and across the savannah. They, too, like those other five bleeding marks, can be the symbols of a people's salvation.

This morning I shall take the red road to Bodou. The men will not go out to work to-day and the women will be waiting. At the entry to the village, the choir will be singing as my old Chevrolet trundles by. That is the traditional welcome. When I first saw it my eyes welled with tears. I saw them there waiting for the Word of God. Here was the realization of all I had imagined: the people waiting for the Book to be opened. Indeed, this is the District which took up the cry: " Send somebody to read to us the Book." The Church has sent me. I have answered the call. I have come to read to them the Book. After a year in the forest the missionary has need of somebody to read the Book to him.

To sit in the Secretary's office in the Missionary Society's

headquarters is to know something of the spiritual alti-
tudes one can touch as the story of Africa's great need is
unrolled by one who has served half a lifetime in the dark
continent. I sat there listening. Yes, this is the work for
me; pushing through the forest and suddenly coming
upon the village where people are hungering and thirsting
after righteousness; sitting in the canoe with boys paddling to the rhythm of their songs, and, as the sun goes
down, landing on the narrow beach where the folk are
already assembled to hear the old, old story; sitting under
the shady palm tree and talking to the little children.

"Yes, send me there, O Lord. Let me serve Thee in
serving them."

I know now that these are the people who have called
me a liar, who have accused me of taking their money
for my own private use, who believed I was a polygamist
because I had been seen out with my wife and a lady missionary. These are they who left me alone in a canoe
except for one small youth; who promised to call for me
to row me to a village on the other side of the lagoon,
and arrived too late to make the journey worth-while.
These are the people who now tell me how discouraged
they are if I get to their villages late.

Yet if Lepri would only come back from market I
would get off on my way to Bodou; I would set out
gladly to be with them. The five red gashes seem to
stretch out to the uttermost need of these people and
challenge me to follow.

There came, of course, that phase common to most
missionaries, a period of revulsion, when I despised them,
thinking I saw through their little hypocrisies and their
double-meaning phrases. I was disgusted by their mock

piety and their immorality. Even the way they ate shocked me. I would watch them covertly as they ate with gaping mouths, sucking their greasy fingers with every fistful of food they picked out of the common bowl. They pray with fervour but are faithless. They have no respect for privacy, so that even the simple process of going to bed often became a problem. To shout at them is useless. They will laugh and come back. Then, when the moon gets up, they go off to their houses, and the sins they do by two and two they shall pay for one by one.

After six months in the Ivory Coast I had qualified for a Pharisee.

"Look at them," I would mutter: "they live like animals and are as free of inhibitions. I thank, Thee, Lord, that I am not as one of them."

After six years with them I want to take my stand alongside the publican. It is not that they have changed. I am like the photographer who suddenly finds his niche in portraiture; he sees the subject and loves him for what he is. Against this backcloth of disadvantage, suffering and fear, these people stand out like saints. Time catches them in the act of climbing towards eternity, and he who crawls a hundred feet out of a pit has gone just as far as he who climbs the same distance up a cliff.

I can see the red road at the bottom of the hill. It winds along the side of the lagoon and turns left at the oil factory and is lost in the bush. A few women are straggling along on their way home to Kpass. Another little group is waiting for a lorry to take them to Bouboury. At the end of that road the people at Bodou are waiting for me. Just as they wait in the shops, in the offices, in the markets, so they wait for me. And I wait for Lepri.

III

"WHERE have you been all this time? Does it take an hour and five minutes to buy five francs' worth of *atieki*?"

"Monsieur, there's a woman just outside Perinaud's and she's collapsed."

That is just like Lepri, the crafty rascal. He introduces a catastrophe when we are dealing with other matters, hoping that in the general confusion his own short-comings will be overlooked.

"I think you ought to go down and take her to the hospital, monsieur."

"Aren't there any vans standing in the market? I'm over an hour late as it is and the hospital is not in my direction."

To this argument there is no reply. Lepri clambers on to the seat beside me and waits.

" It's all very well," I continue, half to myself, " but these people think I'm at their beck and call, that they have only to send up a boy and I will go running down to help them out of their trouble. They forget that I have other things to do."

I look at Lepri. He is dipping his fingers into the banana leaf full of *atieki* and carrying a few grains to his mouth.

" And how many times have I told you not to make a mess in my van? " I cry. " How many times have I told you not to eat that stuff when you are with me? "

Why they take the trouble, and waste hours, in turning good manioc into this dry smelly stuff is quite beyond me. I detest it.

Lepri says: " I didn't find out whether she was Catholic or Protestant."

Of all the irrelevant people Lepri is the chief, unless he knows instinctively that a soft answer turns away wrath. I let in the clutch slowly and the van begins to jolt down the hill. As I turn the corner by the Church I can see right down into the market with Perinaud's on the left. A crowd of people has gathered there, a crowd which soon becomes aware of my arrival. I drive up to the side of the shop and there I see the woman who has collapsed. She is fat and boneless and her body is lolling on the shoulder of a young man who sits on the step and wipes her face with a dirty handkerchief.

" Who are you? " I ask the young man.

" A nephew," he replies.

The woman's eyes are closed, her breathing is heavy.

" Has she been ill long? "

" Never known her ill before," the young man answers.

I look round on the crowd. Every face shows concern mingled with fear. They would not touch this woman as she is.

"Let's get her into the back of the van," I say, but I know it is the nephew and myself who will have to do the lifting. I take hold of her legs and Lepri is pressed into service to help the nephew at the other end.

"Stand back, you chumps," I shout to the people crowding around the van. With a struggle we prop up this half-naked body against my trekking boxes. I fasten the tailboard and go to start the engine. But no, before I can get away I must speak again to the people. Quite a number of them are trying to get in with the patient to see the sequel to the story. I take hold of a foot which is sticking up over the tailboard. It belongs to a youth.

"Are you a relative?" I ask.

"No, monsieur."

"Well, what are you doing in my van? Get out."

Of a woman I ask: "Are you ill, too, Mammy?"

"No, Papa."

"Well, why be carried to the hospital? Out you go!"

It takes ten minutes to get the people out and away from the almost suffocated patient. I get hold of the wheel and drive off, smiling and waving to the people I have just bullied and shouted at. And they laugh and wave and send me on my way with salutations and joy.

The Government hospital at Dabou is a dispensary with a maternity ward attached. Expectant mothers, sitting on the ground just inside the gate, wave to us as we turn into the yard. The lady in the back of the van has regained consciousness and is looking round, alarmed to find herself riding with a European. A male nurse helps her to get out and together we go to see the doctor. He is a man of forty years, and, like most native doctors in this country, is not a fully qualified practitioner. The French have made a brave attempt to combat disease. Every government centre has its medical auxiliary. But there is still a good deal to be done. The need is for closer supervision of the work.

This doctor smiles and bows. He is a native of French Sudan. He assures me he will soon get the lady well, mutters something in a language I do not understand, and walks away. As he is going, I call after him: " Shall I wait? " He answers over his shoulder that it is not necessary.

I begin a tattoo on the self-starter, stamp on the accelerator, and think of the good lady now being treated in the dispensary. Is she being treated? Is she being told by the nurse that she will have to pay a hundred francs before she can see the doctor? Has she already paid up? Perhaps I should have stayed with her to stop any nonsense of that sort. But I know she prefers to be alone, even if it costs her extra. She reminds me of Samuel Nomel, who had yaws, and asked me for an advance on his salary so that he could go to the hospital.

" But medical attention is free," I said.

" I know," he answered, " but in practice we have to pay."

" You HAVE to pay? "

" Well, no, you don't have to, but those who do are served first, and the more you pay the quicker you get in to see the doctor."

" Who asks for the money? "

" Nobody asks," he replied with a worried smile.

"It's . . . it's like going to see somebody very important; you take him a gift so that he will think kindly of you."

"And you give the nurses something to make them think kindly of you?"

"Are you getting angry with me, monsieur?"

"No, I just want to know how you pay this money to people who do not ask for it."

"Well," he said, "I go into the waiting-room and there are a lot of us there. In a few moments the nurse puts his head round the door and I beckon him. I give him a hundred francs, which he takes, and disappears. The next time he looks in the waiting-room I shall know if I have paid him enough, because, if I have, I shall be called first. If he calls another, and I am in a very great hurry to be served, then I must try with another hundred francs."

"And if you don't pay?"

"Well, I wait there until all the others have been seen, and if there is a lot I may have to return the next day."

"But don't you think that is wrong?" I ask.

"Monsieur," he replied, shrugging his shoulders in typical French fashion, "you may think it is wrong but for us, ' les noirs,' we live like that and we cannot change it."

"But if all the people were Christians you would not have to live like that and you would all be willing to wait your turn in the doctor's queue."

"You are right, monsieur; if we were all Christians everything would be different, but, you see, we are not."

IV

It is impossible to avoid the hole which stretches across the hospital exit, and as the car lurches and shudders, I wonder if I shall finish my journey without the usual breakdown.

I always drive slowly through the main street at Dabou, for, apart from the swarms of people who are as indifferent as deaf mutes to the danger of the traffic, there is always the stray pig or goat who decides to cross from the safety of one side of the road to the other just as I am passing.

At the end of the street there is a signpost indicating Lahou to the left and the Administrator's residence to the right. Still crawling along, I turn onto the Bodou Road and smell the sweet odour of palm-oil. Steam escapes from a rusty exhaust-pipe in the wall of the factory. This particular building produces soap, thick yellow-brown bars stamped with the image of a lion and the words: "*Fabriqué à Dabou.*" We are proud of our factory and talk amongst ourselves of the industrialisation of Africa as though we personally were its pioneers.

But the pyramids will never again be a mystery to me after seeing this factory built. The great machines, piled high upon platforms built just under the gables, were manœuvred into position by Africans straight from the bush, who could not tell the difference between a spanner and a screwdriver. The great boilers, now taken so much for granted, were raised and fixed by about thirty men who swarmed all round them, clutching here and there for a good hold on the slippery black steel. The foreman, a man called Braïma, led his men expertly.

"Take hold," he would cry, and, when every muscle was taut, he would shout: "He!" to which his men would echo "HE!" Three times he would cry: "He!" to the resounding answer, and then all would lift and push, crying: "Brrrrrrrrrrrrrrrrrrrrrrrrrrrrrrrrrp!"

The factory is running to-day, thanks to those men with the knotted veins under wet, black skins, who strained as they cried: "He! HE! He! HE! He! HE! Brrrrrrrrrrrrrrrrrrrrrrrrrrrrrrrp!"

I climb the hill on the other side of Kpass and glimpse the savannah through the breaks in the hedge. The engine coughs, splutters and stops.

"Out of petrol," says Lepri, opening his mouth for the first time since I told him about eating *atieki* in the van.

Before I can answer, he is out, and trying to force open the bonnet with a screwdriver.

"Not that way, stupid. There is a right and wrong way for doing everything," I tell him heavily.

He grins and says nothing, which shows he is not listening. Inspection reveals plenty of petrol in the tank. I take a few bits and pieces out of the carburettor and blow through them as I have seen mechanics doing, and put them back. I have lost the box spanner for the plugs, so I cannot check them over. I straighten my back just as Lepri decides that it is the petrol pump which is not working.

"You'll say it's a puncture next," I answer.

I lean against the hot mudguard and think, but, unless the fault is of the classical type one finds explained in car-owners' handbooks, thinking is as poor as guessing. This is dirty work, and I wipe my greasy hands on a greasier rag, and Lepri tells me that my face is as dirty as my shorts. When I get home, Helen will ask what I have been doing to get my clothes in such a condition.

"Other men don't get into that state," she says.

But other men, perhaps, haven't cars like mine. It is easy for her sitting there at home teaching a handful of ministerial students a little English. She doesn't see what I have to put up with. And, if Lepri had a little more sense, he would be able to lend a hand. He is sitting patiently by the roadside. He looks up and smiles, and I feel I have betrayed his good name by harbouring such ugly thoughts about him.

It's a good job Helen is a missionary, too. It is possible, I suppose, for a wife not to be called to the Mission field. A plumber's wife need only serve as a mate in the strict sense of the word, but a missionary's wife must take part in her husband's job. Her attitude affects his.

I put another stone behind the rear wheel, for the parking brakes have never worked, and there is not a garage here which can do an effective overhaul of them.

It is very hot. If I thought I was going to be here long, I would open the chop-box and get out a flask of tea. Lepri is singing. I sometimes wonder if Africans sing because they are happy, or if, like the birds, they cannot help themselves.

In the distance a cyclist is ringing his bell incessantly, and I look up, expecting to see an African dressed in his best clothes hurtling down the hill towards Babou. Instead, I see an African in dirty overalls braking his machine to a standstill as he sees us *en panne* by the roadside.

" Can I help you, monsieur ? "

" That depends on whether you know anything about cars."

" I'm a mechanic," he says proudly. " You're from the Mission, aren't you ? "

" Yes, but how did you know ? "

" 'Seen you in the villages."

" Good. Are you a Christian ? "

" Certainly. I'm a Catholic. We are going to buy the Pope a television."

" That's fine."

" What is a television, monsieur ? "

" It's a machine which will help you to see and hear the Pope speaking—but that is for the future."

" Is it like the cinema ? "

" Yes, a bit."

" But it costs a lot more."

" I expect it does."

He looks at the engine and suggest all the faults which Lepri and I have shared between us before his arrival.

" Well, if it isn't any of those things," he says finally, " it is the coil."

He puts his hand on it and shakes his head: " I told you so. It should never be as hot as that. Your coil has gone— that's what has happened—your coil has gone. If you like I will take your boy on the bicycle to Dabou and he can buy you a new one."

I give Lepri a thousand franc note and offer a couple of hundred to the good Samaritan.

" Not from you, monsieur," he says. " If it was any- body else I would ask for more, but I never take anything from the Mission."

As I put the two hundred francs back into my pocket the mechanic wobbles away with Lepri sitting on the crossbar. I sit on the running-board and take the cork out of the flask.

V

It seems incongruous, but the African stands astride the centuries. He tells me I need a new coil for my engine, and then, very likely, cycles home to take his daughter to the fetisher. In one breath he will talk of television for the Pope and the clairvoyance of the sorcerers. To him both are facts.

There was Etienne Sokroi the night I sat outside his hut in the light of a tin hurricane lamp. We were talking of the mission and the work of God, when into the conversation he threw: " Do you hear them in the forest, monsieur ? "

" Hear what ? " I asked.

" The spirits and the little folk."

I looked across the patch of light and saw his big head outlined against the limewashed wall. The whites of his eyes were whiter than fact.

" Do you hear them, then ? " I parried.

" I'm asking you," he said stubbornly.

" Well, no," I replied, " I do not hear them."

" That's because you have other voices," he said, " but when I hurry through the forest at dusk, they call me and I feel them brush by my head, because they, too, are hurrying."

" What do they say ? " I asked.

" Ah, monsieur, I don't wait to listen. I can't tell you what they say, but they speak."

" Have you seen them ? "

" No, I have never seen them, but there are many people in the village who have."

" Perhaps they are like the little folk who used to live in the English forests," I said. " They stand in the woods at dusk, and, as you pass by, they call and beckon you to follow them—and if you obey, you are lost."

The whites of Etienne's eyes became larger.

" That's just what they do here," he spluttered.

" I know," I replied, " and when you hear the voices which you say I hear, you will no longer hear the little folk enticing you away."

Etienne stretched himself and yawned.

" Perhaps you are right," he said, " but you must excuse me now for an hour or so, because I have to clean and oil my brother's coffee-grinding machine."

So he stepped out of the night of primitive Africa into the night of the twentieth century with its coffee grinding machines and thousand franc notes. He moves from one to the other with amazing facility, but he would do better with more light.

My problem, like that of all missionaries in this country, is to know how to lead these people away from the old ways, on the one hand, and the spell of the new on the other, to that real life which is in Christ Jesus. How difficult that is can only be appreciated by those who live here. Say to a man like Etienne, for example, that there are no spirits in the forest, and he will reply: " But I've heard them."

He is always hearing them. They are as real to him as this tea, which is scalding my mouth, is to me.

" But they can't be real, Etienne; they can't be real." Just tell him that, and he will look at you pityingly and ask you how one can refute a fact.

The whole fabric of their lives is woven around this belief. The belief is imprisoned in the tribal heart. Sometimes it is almost stifled, more often it throws god-fearing men to the ground like folk possessed and crying for mercy from a half-derided faith. The European can scorn the primitive beliefs of a people, but African Christians have a greater respect for this thing which can cut down the faithful as surely as a flash of lightning cuts down a tree. Perhaps they have never really measured the power of Grace against the ancient power.

" Give them Christ," we are told. " Preach the Gospel. He will set the prisoner free." And He does. It is slow work and a lifetime of faith can be built on a misconception. That is why, here, more than anywhere else, a miracle happens every time a man, set free, comes staggering home to God.

On the other hand, there is the power of the almighty franc. In one village close to Abidjan we were greeted by a young man from the Gold Coast. He came straight into the room where we were lodging, and presented Helen with a bottle of warm lemonade.

" Dis is for you, Mudder," he said quickly, " dis is for you. I come heah; I make plenty money and then I go back home one time. Take it, Mudder. You bring me luck and I make plenty money."

The good Samaritan just now refused the two hundred francs. He is a rare case. Alone in the Adzopé forest with a weak battery, I was at a loss to know how to get the car moving. It needed half a dozen lusty men to push it for a few yards. There were a dozen such fellows at hand. They were felling trees and I called to them for help. They looked and laughed.

" How much will you pay us" they asked from their cutting platforms.

A man is in trouble. They see he cannot move, and they trade on his helplessness. To take a snapshot, to get a tyre pumped, to ask a simple favour, one has to haggle over a price to be paid, unless one finds a good Samaritan. These people have quickly learned that the little chits of coloured paper have a value far in excess of their appearance. Money is magic, money changes man, money is big power.

Our mission has its share of members educated to the general standard of the country, the standard required for work in offices and Government departments. Some of these members are attracted by the work in the Mission, but sickened by the wages paid. But one feels that the majority would never be satisfied with the best the Mission could pay, if it fell short of that paid by big business.

The five red roads symbolize the African Calvary, for He saves them from what they were and is crucified by what they become. Perhaps a little footpath to the fetish shrine has disappeared, but the great red *Via Dolorosa* has taken its place.

But he never leaves Himself without a remnant, the faithful few, whom the successful deride for their faith in poverty, believing it a greater sacrifice than their own poverty of faith.

Will Lepri be amongst this little band? I can hear him now, singing his way along the road with my new coil:

> " A Dieu seul j'abandonne
> Ma vie et ma personne
> Mes projets et mes voeux . . ."

Who can tell? When he leaves school he will very likely go the way of so many others, despite the sentiments of his song. With a few educated young men dedicated to Christ's cause, more people could be led out of the darkness. And the end would be more incongruous than the position to-day, for the tribe would straddle across the ages of time and the aeons of eternity. They would be at one and the same time the children of yesterday and the sons of the everlasting.

VI

" Pass me the adjustable spanner, Lepri, and we shall be off in a few minutes."

The coil is bolted into position, the bonnet closed, and I press the starter fearfully. The mechanic was right; the coil was faulty.

The old car grumbles up the remainder of the hill and hums down the other side toward Bouboury and the forest. Men have been working here. A patch of bush bordering the forest has been cleared. All the tropical creeper, in deadly conflict with half-suffocated shrubs, has been cut back, and piled in heaps, to serve as rope in house construction. The earth in this new clearing is the colour of old blood. A few tall cotton trees lift their grey, bleached bodies, like soldiers drained of life in the act of surrender. In a few weeks manioc will be growing here, where once reigned that tropical chaos, the bush. The primary forest has long since gone, but growth is easy and

27

quick. In a matter of months an empty native house will collapse in ruins, succumbing to the ever-challenging bush.

The road enters the tunnel which is the forest, and there is twilight at midday, and a strange quiet, broken only by the hum of the car and an occasional piping from an Allied Hornbill as it flaps its clumsy way from one branch to another.

This is Africa, the Africa of the story books, where a million fears are born and cherished. Standing between two trees is a man, hardly perceptible against the dark background. He becomes a half-truth one hasn't the time to explore. To stop the car, to return to see if it really was a man or an illusion, is a waste of time. One sees things in the forest. Instead of naked truth, one has to make do in this half-light with imagination dressed up. And what a dress it is! It was this queer twist to imagination which interrupted my daydreams that day I returned from Armebé. The canoe was drifting with the current, save for the occasional dip of the steersman's paddle. The forest rose up dense on either bank. A cry behind brought us to a halt in mid-river, and alongside came one of the most muscular men I have ever seen, and one of the most frightened. He had to collect some fishing gear which he had left on the edge of the river, but he was afraid to go alone.

" There's a wild animal there, monsieur."

" What kind of wild animal, a leopard? "

" No, worse than that, but I do not know what it is called."

" Describe it, then."

" It is black and has the head of a lion, with long hair falling down over its eyes. It has the shoulders of a dog, which taper away to the hind-quarters of a monkey."

" And what kind of tail has it? " I asked, jokingly.

" It is the stringy tail of a pig," was the prompt reply.

He had seen it; his friends had seen it. Women were not allowed to go for water unaccompanied, but such an animal never existed.

" You are a Christian, aren't you? " I asked, as we stood on the river bank.

" Indeed I am," he replied. " I'm a full member."

" Then you must trust Christ when you see that animal again and pronounce the benediction over it, and it will trot off, and you will never see it again."

" Yes," he answered meekly, but when I looked back again from the middle of the river, he was paddling away from the danger zone we had just left as fast as his great knotty arms would allow.

The forest is in the blood of the people. It speaks a language they understand and they learn its songs. They sing with an uncanny rhythm, the volume of which fades and grows to a roar. One can almost imagine the rain beating on the hard tropical leaves and the wind blowing in gusts across the tops of the branches. David heard the sound of marching in the tops of the mulberry trees. Paul surely must have had the forest in mind when he wrote: " To this day we know that the entire creation sobs and sighs with pain."

And the forest speaks to this people. Even the word they have chosen for the cross is " tree." That is the tree which will save them from their fears, which will speak a word of peace instead of the whispered horror. It is about this tree I must speak when I get to Bodou. I must tell them about the new Adam, the new Eden and the new tree.

VII

THIS road leads directly to Bouboury, and one gets the impression that it must pass right through the village, or stop dead at the first native threshold. But, just at the entrance, the road takes a sharp turn to the left. One catches a glimpse of our church in the main street. It has a small tree growing out of the roof. Six years ago it was just a tiny plant growing out of the brickwork and I told them: " Better get it down now, before it starts to give you trouble."

They smiled and nodded. Some of them even said that they would get up on the roof one day, but that day has not arrived. Now, several tiles have been pushed aside and fissures have appeared in the wall. A whole corner of the building is threatened, but the danger does not appear imminent to the members. One day they will send a deputation to tell me that a great wedge of the church has fallen into the road.

There is one thing which would most certainly make them act, but there is no sign of that happening. Where the road turns away to Bodou stands the Catholic church, or rather, what will be the Catholic church one day when the priest can sufficiently arouse his lethargic members. For many years now it has presented the same aspect— four red walls of laterite stone with gaping holes where the windows and doors will be fixed. Here the Catholics worship twice a day, but they are never moved to finish the work they have started.

The Protestants watch them in a self-satisfied way. "They haven't the means," they say; "they are weak, whereas we have a big church, a permanent building and a bell weighing nearly forty kilos."

The day will come when the Catholics will shake themselves, and the African masons will come along with their rickety scaffolding, and the old men in the Protestant church will shake their heads and say: "They must not build a better church than ours. We must start a renovation fund—if necessary, a rebuilding fund."

And if on that day the tree in the roof has not overturned the coping stones, somebody will be sent up at once to dig it out.

The most modern building in Bouboury is also found on the outskirts of the village. It is the new regional school. The Chief of Bouboury is a Protestant. He is very young to be Chief. When he came to office he set to work to build a school and found half the cost from amongst his people.

" It's a fine school, Chief," I said to him one day.

" Yes," he replied haughtily, " it's a fine school, and it is our school. We have waited and waited for the Mission to build us a school and to teach our children, but now we have lost patience. We do not need you any more."

Tell him that there are ninety villages in the circuit and all want schools, and he will not listen. Ask him why he thinks Bouboury should get special treatment, and he lifts his chin in disdain and turns his head. Tell him that it is no good building schools unless we can get the staff, and he clicks his tongue at the back of his throat, which is the African way of saying: " Nonsense."

The fact is the Mission has only been able to open four schools for the whole of the Ivory Coast, and two of them are already closed. We cannot afford to repeat in Bouboury what has happened in Lahou. There, on the beach almost, is the little chapel and the school building with its six round-topped windows, like six eyebrows raised in consternation because of the sniggering Catholics who talk of another Protestant fortress falling into ruin, and because the Protestants have left such a smart little building to become a wreck.

" You have abandoned your people here," says the French Administrator. " Why don't you open your school? There are hundreds of children longing for a little education."

And the Chief at Bouboury says his people have lost patience, and cannot wait any longer for the Mission to educate their children!

There are different opinions concerning the Church's part in education. The Ivory Coast presents a task too great for the Mission to tackle. It should select. To ensure future workers in the Mission it should have, in a few strategic centres, efficient schools. It should spend what money it can devote to this side of its work in doing something decent, if only in a small way. Men like the Chief at Bouboury will never understand. They will not accept the fact that the future of education in the French colonies is in the hands of the Government. As one French missionary put it: " The Protestant minority in France and overseas has nothing to lose, and everything to gain, in Government-controlled education."

We shall not lose the children at Bouboury because they are attending a government school. As long as we can give them religious instruction we shall keep them. They need it. They have not the same inspiration their fathers received from the preaching of Prophet Harris. There is old Joseph Latro at Bouboury, who was baptised by Harris, and remains faithful amidst the changing scene. He gave testimony against his daughter when she was charged with adultery.

" She is a bad girl, always has been; and though she is flesh of my flesh, I cannot deny it. What her husband says is true. I have tried to help her, but she will not listen to me."

The daughter of Joseph Latro did not know the Prophet Harris. She grew up on the fervour of a past generation, before the Church realized the value of religious education. She has all the marks of a Christian without the spirit. She is always in church, is a member of the singing band, and pays her church dues regularly. She reminds me of the boy I saw in Abidjan the day after the boxing match arranged between the middle-weight

33

champions of the Ivory Coast and the Gold Coast. I saw this lad in the school playground shadow boxing. He had all the actions off to perfection. Dancing on his toes, he would lash out at his imaginary opponent with all the classical straights and hooks, and would dodge to avoid blows aimed at him. Then, suddenly, another schoolboy came into the playground. He was bigger and stronger. He saw the would-be boxer, and going straight up to him, smacked his face and walked on. All the defence and dancing and doging had been so much sham. He had the movement without the reason, the manner without the science.

How can one show these people what is of true value, what is real and what is imitation? They must learn now life's great values before experience shows them as rudely as a slap on the face.

VIII

"THAT'S Abraham Amari ahead," said Lepri, pointing
to a solitary traveller about half a mile down the road.

"How do you know from this distance?" I asked.

"Tell by his walk."

As the van draws nearer I, too, can see it is Amari—not
by his walk, but by his hat. He wears a fawn-coloured
trilby and a native cloth. There are many who thus mix
European with African dress, but with Amari it always
seems slightly comic.

The car slows down, and Amari greets me.

"Where are you going, monsieur?"

"To Bodou."

"Then perhaps you could give me a lift as far as
Mopoyem."

" That is why I have stopped."

Lepri moves over toward me to make room for Amari. I like the name Amari; it is such a gentle sound, and this man is like his name. It is given only to children born after twins. All Adjukru names run in an established order. One is named according to one's place in the family.

Amari takes off his trilby hat. He is happy to be riding.

" How is the church? " I ask.

" It's going along fine. You remember we were putting on the roof the last time you were there? Well, it's finished now. I am glad the people took your advice and bought asbestos for the roof instead of tiles."

It was Amari who acted as spokesman when the idea of building a permanent Church was raised. It was he, too, who suggested that all the money collected be kept in the Circuit safe, and he is happy that every franc paid in has been well guarded.

I take a quick glimpse of him sitting beside Lepri. He is half smiling with contentment. He has a fine, honest face. It is the face of a Christian. But is he? Can one ever be sure of these people? Shall I hear next week that this man has gone off to see the fetisher?

The road gets bad here. Traffic, too heavy for the surface, has cut deep ruts in it. The trees and grass on the roadside are powdered with red dust thrown up by the lorries, forcing an artificial autumn on a thick primeval world which is loath to die. The Ivory Coast is like that to-day. The old has a dying air along the highways of civilization, but, push back into the bush, and one comes face to face with customs and practices which have defied the passing centuries. They live on, enshrined in well-handled pieces of wood, in charms, in words, in fingers pointed in accusation and in the low throbbing of the drums. It is here that Jacques Adangba came to die. The dispensary could do nothing for him.

" Give him to us," said the people. " We know what is wrong with him and why he is ill." His cure was death.

It is here that one of our local preachers, accused of murdering his nephew, drank the fetish potion and fell on his back in terrible agony, and by the same potion was restored to himself after promising to quit the Mission.

In this same bush the soul of one of our catechist's children was eaten. The catechist was not in the village at the time. The child was staying with her grandmother. She fell sick. An old man commented on the fact, and said the child would die, and, pointing out three people, ordinary simple village folk, said they were eating the soul of the little girl. The same old man gave the moment when the last breath left the child's body. Before the grandmother had noticed anything wrong, before the women had started to wail, this old man, sitting under a tree, said to the catechist's sister: " The little one has just passed away." And she had.

It is difficult to tell if the three people, or the old man, or all of them together were responsible for this death.

In that milieu one can see the farmer coming home after a day's hunting. He carries a rifle, the accoutrement of the twentieth century. But, even with the rifle in his hand, the smile will freeze on his face if he hears that somebody is killing him by magic. A wild animal can be shot, but what can be done about magic? In this same milieu one finds the Christian Church.

" We wrestle not against flesh and blood, but against principalities and powers," says Paul. The African can give the same testimony. The missionary, baffled, turns to his most trustworthy worker and learns that he has become a renegade. He turns to Christ and learns to use what little faith is shown by the people as a spear to strike harder at the enemy.

Ernest Akpa, the local preacher at Ngati, came like that. " Come to the village one night and I will show you one of your members who is leading away the people by sorcery."

I went. At about ten-thirty at night I was taken to a distant compound, and there I saw her, a member on trial, dancing and prophesying. Around her were about forty people, hypnotised and dancing convulsively. As I watched her, with her head thrown back in abandon and her lips parted, I wished that Jesus had been there in the flesh instead of me.

" How did she get like that? " I whispered.

" She claims to have eaten the flesh of a dead baby," the preacher answered, " and now she can sway all these people."

It is against this sort of thing the Cross must prevail. It is to these people one must take the Christ. Only He can cleanse this kind, only He can get behind this false autumn, the mock modernisation of the highway, to the fear-infested depths. Yet it is by this modern highway that He must go to those who need Him. It must become more than ever, God's red road.

A few people are waiting at the cross-roads as though expecting me to set down Amari. Amongst them is old Bernard Akmel, the leper. He stands there amongst the rest as though he were clean. The common belief that lepers are, and always have been, segregated, is not true. Jesus himself once had supper with a leper. Old Bernard, too, wanders about the village without having to shout " Unclean, unclean." His wife, I hear, has now become a leper—caught it off him, I suppose. But what is the alternative? Where can he go for help? Who will take him in if the village casts him out? In any case he will disintegrate, like the old lady at Tiassalé to whom I gave Communion for the last time.

" Take and drink this in remembrance . . ." I said, and then realized that she had no fingers with which to take it, no eyes to see what she was taking, and a mouth twisted and decayed, so that one could merely moisten what once were human lips. God has never asked for human sacrifice, much less this kind.

Old Bernard stands there blinking at me pathetically. He gives me a small bunch of bananas, which I take with thanks, but, as I pass down the road to Bodou, I quietly drop them out of the window.

IX

I SHALL be glad to arrive, to take the kettle off the primus and to smell the fresh tea as the steam escapes out of the teapot.

Lepri hears the choir before I do, and joins in with his usual gusto. And then I catch the first glimpse of them waiting in the hollow. How long have they been waiting there, I wonder—at least three hours. These are the people of whom I have pastoral care. I have sixteen thousand like them and not a black sheep amongst them, not even the villains. They seem as glad to see me as I am to see them, and they wave as the car draws closer. It is the old formation I have come to know so well. The young girls and women are in front, each armed with two handkerchiefs to wave as they sing and dance.

Behind, is the solid phalanx of men, those who sing like men and those who rumble deep as thunder. Amongst the latter is a tall singer, wearing two hats, one on top of the other. He is taking his job very seriously, for, although they are singing: " O for a thousand tongues to sing," he is looking very melancholy, a feeling he tries to impart to his neighbours on either side by turning from one to the other and singing in their ears, and raising his great eyes to heaven. He is very likely a clown, a serious-faced comedian. He knows I am looking at him and his hats, but he shows no sign of recognition.

Suddenly I am reminded of the ship riding at anchor just off Lomé in Togoland. The night before had been Twelfth Night and there had been a great spirit of carnival amongst the French passengers. Roman priests were sitting at table wearing paper hats, charms from the cake were being thrown across the saloon and kisses claimed in return.

All that passed with the night. The morning had come and the passengers, after the meagre French breakfast, were leaning over the side of the ship watching the cargo being taken off. Below, a huge barge was rising on the swell and inside it were four African stevedores. They were looking up and joking with the passengers. Then somebody threw down a paper hat which had been used in the Twelfth Night celebrations. This was followed by more hats and squeakers. The Africans were delighted, and, with the coloured hats on their heads and the squeakers in their mouths, they began capering round the barge.

A lady standing next to me turned and said: " They are just like little children, aren't they."

I replied: "Yes, almost as juvenile as we were last night."

It is a common fallacy to think that, because the African is a past master at clowning, he is childish. Africans have always the carnival under their skin. Life is too tragic to have anything else. What we do once or twice a year to brighten the dreary scene, they put on every time the moon is full and riding its silver way over the grey thatched roofs of the village.

He wears two hats, this bass singer in the Bodou choir. And why should he not?

The choirmaster speaks to me through the car window. "Will you go along slowly now because the members want to lead you in."

"Ah, good! Let them get on then, eh! I am very late as it is."

They move off now. The men with their backs to me are jogging forward. They are singing "Man of Sorrows, What a name." The tempo is considerably increased and they are all dancing to this dirge-like hymn. They instinctively know and understand the contrast of the words. "Man of Sorrows" is not good enough for this Jesus—"Hallelujah, what a Saviour!"

There are people waiting at every little alley to see the procession, and then old Samson comes striding toward us with his long stick.

I stop the car.

"Good day to you, Monsieur Samson. How are you? Well?"

"A little, monsieur, just a very little."

Rarely will these people admit good health.

"Ça va?"

" *Ah, ça va un petit peu.* "

The rest-house for the missionary has been swept out. A cloth has been put on the table, and a bottle, bearing a Booth's dry gin label, holds a few flowers already drooping because they have been suffocated in the narrow neck of the bottle.

In this house a raffia mat has been hung up to make a partition, which allows me the privilege of a separate bedroom.

All my boxes are piled in the dining-room section which is crowded with people. There is a lot of noise and I am getting hotter. The crowd outside, which cannot get in, begins to shout. There is a surging of people near me, and through the door is squeezed Albert Metchro, the catechist. He is still wearing his navy blue, open cellular vest tucked into his khaki shorts. He is fat. He is too fat. I can see the three horizontal ridges which serve as his neck. He is grumbling as he comes.

" *Bonjour*, monsieur," he says, puffing. " I did not hear you come."

Old Samson says: " Albert, ask the white man for his news."

" Monsieur," says Albert, " they ask you for your news."

I tell them that I am on trek and that this is my first village since I left Dabou. They knew I was coming. I am sorry to be late, but at Dabou I had to take a lady to hospital who had fallen ill in the road, and then on the way the car fell ill, and Lepri had to return to Dabou for spares. But I am glad to be with them. I hope they have peace in the village.

Albert interprets this and then gives me Samson's reply.

43

There was nothing serious to report. They knew I would be arriving to-day, but, after waiting at the road from six this morning, many of them had gone home discouraged. But all were happy now that I had arrived.

I shake hands with all the men and sit down.

"Simn Gô," says Samson, and the crowd begins to disperse.

Now I am alone. I pull off my shirt and wipe my arms on a towel. Lepri has opened the chop-box, the primus is roaring in the corner, and I step behind the raffia partition to put up my camp bed. There is a tiny window about a foot square with a shutter made of palm cane. I open this and look out.

The little window looks on to another compound. A young girl of fourteen is pulping tomatoes with a large smooth stone. Her legs are slightly apart and her shoulders drawn up. With quick movements of the wrists she brings to bear on this common task all the African rhythm of the ages. The little red cloth hanging down from her naked waist sways to the movement of her body. Here is poetry in movement, and Africans bring this same offering of their whole being to every task, whether it pleases them or not. Nobody pumps a car tyre like the African. Not for him the slow painful compressions of the pump. The rhythm does the job while he thinks of something else, and not only the force of the arms, but the weight of the body is brought down on the pump handle. The pump does not last as long, but what of that?

This girl is gathering up the wet result of her labours into a broken dish. I expect she is a Christian. She turns round as though knowing she is being watched, and treats

44

me to a flashing white smile. She calls out a welcome in one of the eight languages one finds in this circuit. I know only a few words, so I answer in French.

We shall not see real co-ordination of the work here until the people take seriously to French or a predominant African language. Our literacy work is impeded by this great babel. We hear from many quarters that we must teach the people to read. A greater enemy than illiteracy is a literate people without literature. This little girl perhaps cannot read. If she is taught she will be able to read the first primer and Mark's Gospel in her own language. All the other great literature we have inherited is denied this girl, whose every movement has the magic of a fairytale in it. What could she become if she had half of what a European child gets at the same age? Or would sophistication take the crimp out of her hair and the song out of her heart, as it has done for some modern African women along the West Coast of Africa?

At the moment she must be satisfied to stare at the openwork on Albert Metchro's vest as he tells the story of God's way with men. One day, another girl in this village will pulp tomatoes with a smooth stone, and she will put the rhythm of the work to the words of the twenty-third Psalm, which she will read with her own eyes and in her own language, and Erasmus's dream of common man possessing the Word of God will come true once again, and this time in a little village in the backwoods of Africa.

X

HELEN must have put in the potatoes as a surprise. They are certainly a change from the heavy yam, which clings to the palate and becomes a burden after one has got over the novelty of eating it. Manioc is different. Made into rissoles and fried in groundnut oil, it can be quite tasty, though there are some Europeans who will not eat it because they say it is bad for the eyes.

I take a potato out of the water and peel it. They have come from France, but they look as though they have lingered a long time on the way. Most of them are spongy and some rotten, but fried chips with corned beef will make all the difference to me in a few moments.

Two little boys have come to the door and are resting their faces against the lintel. They sniff like European children, and sigh, and change the weight of their bodies from one foot to the other. I wink at them and they offer in exchange a full view of their tiny white teeth. The whites of their eyes are pure white, not tinged with blue like ours, and not tinged with red like their fathers'.

" What do you want ? " I ask.

They look at one another, hold their hands to their mouths and giggle. They do not know what they want, but they will take anything you have to offer.

I open my sugar tin and give them each a piece. This little tradition accomplished, they enter the room and sit down at my feet.

Sugar is not something you pop into your mouth at once. It has to be cherished and warmed in the hand. It has to be licked surreptitiously. Finally, it has to be spread out in the palm of the hand, and mashed with a dirty little finger until it is no longer white. Then, when it is almost liquid, it has to be licked up with determined, upward strokes of the tongue.

As Lepri puts the potatoes into the frying pan, Albert, the catechist, comes in. In his hand is a sheet of paper torn from an exercise book.

" Pardon," he says, as he steps across the threshold, " but I have brought you the list of baptisms."

I take the paper and glance down it. There are twenty-three children to be baptised.

" Are all their parents members ? " I ask.

" Yes, but two have ceased to meet in class."

" And what about those who wish to become full members ? "

" Their names are on the other side of the paper."

Fourteen men and women have had their names written down as wishing to pass the examination. Below this list there are two names apart.

" What are these ? " I ask.

" Those," Albert explains, " are the palavers. Marie

Melm has left her husband and the Church cannot decide who is guilty."

" Have they no idea at all ? "

" They think the woman should be made to return to her husband."

I note that this is not a genuine straight-forward answer and decide to look into the matter from the husband's side.

" Augustin Gremel has become a polygamist."

" That is all—just those two ? What does Augustin's wife think about it ? "

" She says that she will marry another man unless this other woman is sent off."

" All right, Albert, bring in the " on-trial " members for their examination in about an hour's time."

" You want these potatoes before they get burned up, monsieur ? "

" Yes, please, and don't forget the corned beef and the bread."

The bread is quite new. In a few days the remainder will be growing green, and one has to pick out the pieces which have not gone mouldy. A colleague in the next Circuit uses up his mouldy bread in stew. He puts it in a saucepan with a tin of green peas and boils the lot to a pulp. He says it is very tasty, and the colour is the genuine colour of green peas, and does not suggest old bread at all.

But for me just now the chips and the corned beef. I open the door as wide as possible and take my place at the rickety table facing the door. This is not to get a view into the street, but to satisfy native custom, which says that a man who closes his door during a meal or eats with his back to the street, is a gourmand.

XI

A GREAT cry goes up as the first successful candidate leaves. She is an old woman who has tried several times to pass the examination for full membership. I get up to peep through the window, and she is dancing. This is a great moment in her life. To-morrow morning she will be present for Communion.

I sit at the table where Albert, the catechist, is writing notes on the candidates' answers. Lepri is sitting there too, with his head in his hands and his eyes half closed. Before me is a young woman of about twenty years. She is feeding her baby, and smiles nervously as I put the first question.

" What is your name? "

She thinks, searches for a possible catch in this simple question, and then replies slowly: " Dorcas."

" Ah, Dorcas, is there a character in the Bible with that name? "

Without permission, she embarks on the old story, and I listen.

" Is your baby baptised? "

" No."

" Why not? "

" Because my husband is under discipline."

" Do you help your husband? "

" Yes."

" Does he pay you for your work? "

" Yes."

" When was the last time you had palaver with him? "

" I have never been on palaver with him."

" He buys you your clothes? "

" Yes."

" And you never make palaver about that? "

" No, never."

" He is a good husband, then? "

" Yes."

" Repeat the Creed."

She goes through the Creed quickly with her eyes closed.

" You have just said that Jesus is the only Son of God. I thought we were all of us His children."

" So we are."

" Then how is He God's only Son? "

She hesitates. A thousand beads of perspiration have appeared on her brow. She closes here eyes. This is what she had been expecting, no doubt, and after doing so well.

" Didn't I tell you about that last night? " cries Albert, almost starting out of his chair with anger.

" Don't worry her," I say calmly. " Let her take her time."

" You are sure we are God's children ? "

" Yes, quite sure."

" And you believe the Creed when it says that Jesus is God's only Son; well, how do you work that out ? "

The baby begins to kick and cry, and the poor woman struggles to think, and then, she knows! Her face lights up as though she has come into a fortune.

" Jesus," she offers, " is God's real Son, but we are his adopted children."

" Adopted ? "

" Yes, Jesus came into the world to do just that."

" What is your baby's name ? "

" Mary."

" Tell me about a Mary in the Bible."

" Jesus one day came to the house of Mary, and when she saw Him coming, she went into the bedroom and put on her best cloth and sandals and came and sat at his feet to listen to his teaching. But Martha, her sister, was in the market buying fish, and when she came back she went straight into the compound to pound the manioc, until somebody told her that Jesus was in the house. She did not wait to wipe off the manioc which had splashed on to her face, but went straight in and gave Mary a piece of her mind: ' What do you mean by sitting there and leaving me to do all the work, you lazy hussy,' she cried, and there would have been big palaver, but Jesus turned to Martha and said that Mary had chosen the better part."

" And had she chosen the better part ? " I ask.

She replies that she does not know, but it was quite certain that her sympathy was with Martha. The story was told too realistically to have any other meaning.

Africans are realistic. They read into facts conclusions and consequences, which, if a little humorous, are, at least, logical. When the young folk at Treichville enacted *Pilgrim's Progress*, everybody wondered why, when Christian changed his sinful clothes, he put on an oilskin and Wellington boots. Only when he came to cross the Jordan could we see that the producer had had his mind on a happy crossing for the hero.

Dorcas seems a good woman. She is illiterate. There is a Circuit rule that all candidates shall learn to read before being accepted. But how can this young mother be expected to learn to read with a baby on her back, the housework to do, and her part of the plantation to cultivate? Besides, who will teach her to read? The old method takes weeks of close application and repetition, and Albert, who has four villages to control, cannot be in Bodou all the time, even if he felt inclined.

In each village there should be somebody capable of teaching the members to read. And there should be enough literature to make the task of reading worthwhile. We need a school for training these shock troops, voluntary workers who can spend their evenings in their own villages helping folk like Dorcas.

After a few more questions I put a tick against her name, and say: " All right. Come to-morrow morning, and, of course, to-night."

She gets up, almost tumbling over her chair in her excitement to get out and tell the glad news.

" Jacques Djedjro," Albert cries, and a hulking fellow lounges into the room and the next candidate is ready for the ordeal.

XII

" I THINK we can begin," says Albert, the catechist, looking around on the members of the Leaders' meeting.

Since the time when Prophet Harris founded this Ivory
Coast Church there have always been Leaders' meetings.
Originally they consisted of twelve apostles and one
preacher. To-day there are class leaders, most of them
illiterate, who are responsible for giving religious instruction and for collecting class money.

After the opening prayer, Augustin Gramel is brought
in, and I recognize him at once. He is old Samson's son.
Samson is looking into his lap, embarrassed. This is a day
he did not expect to see.

" I have been told that you have two wives," I begin
casually.

" That is not true."

" Tell me the truth, then."

" I have only one wife and everybody here knows it."

I wait for the denial from the leaders, but there is silence.

" How long have you been married to the wife you have now? "

A flicker of a smile plays over his face as he answers: " Six weeks."

" But I thought you were married years ago."

" Ah, that was my last wife."

" She's dead now? "

" No, but she does not live with me."

" Can I suggest that she does not live with you because you will not live with her? "

There is no answer to this.

" Where do you live now? "

" In the new house you saw at the entrance to the village."

" Where does your last wife live? "

" In my old house."

" Ah, I see the plan now. You have taken your new wife to live in the new house, and the old wife stays where she has been all along."

" That's right," he answers, as though I am the greatest thickhead he has ever met.

" But why did you move into the new house with a new wife, and leave your old wife in the old house? "

He is now face to face with the great problem in Africa, a problem easily solved before the arrival of the missionary, a problem which could be easily settled now if people would only mind their own business and stop talking to the white man.

" I have no children," he says quietly.

" How long have you been married ? "

" Ten years."

" And you have taken another wife to have children ? "

" Just that."

" What does your first wife say ? "

" She urged me to find another wife. She said, ' Get another woman, but stop this everlasting taunting.' "

I think of Abraham with Sarah and Hagar, but they seemed to have the Lord on their side, whereas these folk find Him against them; at least, the Church is against them.

" But I have just heard that, if you don't send away your second wife, your first wife will marry another man."

" That's because she is jealous," he answers angrily. " I tell you she told me to take this girl, and now she is pregnant, and will very likely give birth to a child to-night; my wife is jealous, because she knows now that it is she who has stopped me from having a family."

" And your new wife," I say, " your new wife is a member too ? "

" She is a member on trial."

" And you are a full member and the choirmaster. I wondered where you were when I arrived to-day. Well, you see, it is very difficult; you cannot remain in the Church and have two wives. I do not want to begin a long lecture now on why the Church holds it to be wrong, but you have known all along that this palaver would come if you took another wife. You must now make up your mind whether you wish to keep this girl and go out of the Church, or to send her away and re-main in God's great family. Look, there is your old father. He is also the father in this church. He is very upset by what you have done. You have brought shame upon him in his old age. Why not accept the advice of the Church?"

The accused runs a dry tongue over drier lips, and then spits out: "I will keep the woman who gives me children. If you will not accept that, then I will go out." And, turning abruptly away from the meeting, he bounds out of the Church.

I turn to Albert. "Put him under discipline with his second wife."

The leaders now wish to talk. They gabble on and gesticulate, but old Samson remains silent. All the members of this Leaders' meeting have known other times when there would have been no palaver over an affair like this. Native custom upholds the man's right; the Church denies it. This is the great barrier not always recognised by the European. We fancy we are looking at the end of reason, when all the time it is a blank wall, and on the other side are thousands of bewildered Africans who have never made a ladder high enough to see just where we are standing. There is not one member on this Leaders' meeting who really understands why Augustin Gramel has to be put under discipline. It is white man's palaver. The white man talks about love. What is that, if it is not what Augustin Gramel has done? How can one persuade a people of the rightness of monogamy if the approach is different, if the terms used are never defined, or, if defined, not understood by one party because there is nothing to which they can be associated? There are enough arguments to convince every monogamist that he is right, but where is the argument to convince the polygamist he is wrong?

I shall go to bed tonight thinking of that baby which will be born during the hours of darkness. It has been born in sin, says the Christian Church everywhere in the world. It is the answer to man's great need, say the generations of mankind since the time of Abraham.

"And now," I say, trying to smile at the leaders in front of me, "we have to see Marie Helm."

"She's here."

Sitting on a side bench is a woman who looks as though she has come straight from her work in the compound. Round her neck is a piece of dirty string, to which is attached a silver-plated Huguenot cross, the emblem of our Church in this country. She is a woman with a large, humorous mouth, but her eyes are leaden.

"What's this story I've been hearing about you?"

"What story?" she asks, as though ignorant of any charge.

"You have left your husband."

"Oh, that," she says, lifting her chin in typical African disdain.

"Well, let us hear about it."

She begins from the time she was first given in marriage, not to the man who charges her to-day, but to her first husband who was called up for military service and died in North Africa. All the details she can remember come into the story and one has to pick out the wheat from the chaff. The man she now has, paid only ten shillings dowry because she was a widow, and what does he think he can get for that? He is a mean old brute who never turns a hand in the plantation, and expects his wife to do it all. Then, when it comes to the big pay out, instead of keeping his wife in clothes, he harbours all the money for himself like the wretched old miser he is.

She gets this harangue off at full speed, as though she has rehearsed it several times. She laughs, glides across the church, and spits out of the window.

"I don't like people who spit," I tell her. "Would you do that in the Chief's house?"

"Yes," she replies.

"Well, then," I argue, in face of an unexpected answer, "this church belongs to somebody much greater than the Chief and He does not like it."

"That is true," she says, "that is very true."

"She's a liar," cries one old man. "Her husband is a good man."

"Tell him to come here and speak for himself, then," I answer.

We wait a few minutes and the husband enters. He is well over sixty and has what I call a pre-Christian face, an expression one sees on the face of most professional fetishers.

"You don't treat your wife as you should," I say, putting a trial shot.

"That's because she doesn't do her work," he replies.

"You admit then that you do not treat her as you should?"

"I treat her well," he answers quickly, trying to retreat from his former statement.

"If you treat me well," cried Marie Malm, "how do you account for this?" She tugs at the piece of old cloth round her waist, the only clothes she is wearing. "This," she shrieks, "is the last thing he bought me."

"But you must not leave your husband because he

does not buy you things. You must stay with him to help him. Why did you marry him if you did not mean to live with him?"

"I married him because I am a widow and must have somebody to look after me. If he doesn't do that, then I must find somebody who will, in return for the work I give."

"Look," I say patiently, trying to forget the great barrier, "all women who are married must stay with their husbands and be faithful to them. We do not give divorces here: that is not our job. We try to reconcile, and we say that we cannot allow you to leave your husband."

Tears of desperation are standing in her eyes. She rises to her feet and wails. A vein stands out thick on her neck. I feel myself silently accused. She seems to be saying: "Why inflict on me terms which were not in the contract? Why tell me I must love this old dodderer when all he wanted was somebody to work for him? Love? There is marriage for the young people just betrothed, there is marriage for widows, and there is love where you can find it, and all are different."

I cannot bear to look any more at this enraged woman with the tears streaming down her face and on to her breasts. The husband looks an old scoundrel, and I expect he is. But I cannot set myself up as a judge and tell her to leave him. Yet, in telling her to stay with her husband, perhaps I am making a wilder judgment.

"Go home and think about it," I tell her, "and if you are not in your husband's compound by next Saturday, you will be under discipline."

I pick up the books and my fountain pen and almost

run out of the Church. Exasperated and baffled, I stand in the middle of the road and look down the alley alongside the church. A little baby is playing in the muddy ditch. Her feet are covered with slush, and she strikes the earth with a small stick. A small black pig with a very long nose drags its slimy hind quarters to the shade of the hedge, but the little girl goes on beating the earth as though she has found the occupation of a lifetime. If life were just a matter of beating the earth and splashing one's legs in the mud, how simple it would be! But it is so much more complex, and very often so much dirtier.

XIII

AFRICA is the land of semi-blackout. Apart from the big towns there is no modern light. To pass through the streets of Porto Novo, for example, just after sundown, is like passing through fairyland. The women are still there, selling their goods by the light of string dipped in cigarette tins full of oil. The Ivory Coast is less romantic. String dipped in palm oil gives off its own odour, a yellow flame, and a good deal of smoke. Hurricane lamps are popular. I carry one, and do all my evening work by its light. Sometimes in the wealthier churches one has the joy of a pressure lamp, which is given to the missionary to brighten his stay in the village.

Bodou has no such luxury, and I sit looking at my hurricane lamp with its tiny tongue of violet surrounded by the fan of yellow flame. By putting the lamp just behind my right arm I can see to read reasonably well. I have brought a little reading with me, including the *Pilgrim's Progress*. I wander on the delectable mountains with that brave soul, Christian, but I lose interest and think about Helen and what she is doing at this moment. Then I think of the Circuit I left in England to come out here, and I try to place some of the men I knew there in this African setting, and a smile breaks over my face when I think of the utter impossibility of it for some of them. But they were good folk. Their wives did not leave them. They did not own a couple of wives apiece; the nearest they got to thinking that way was when they read Deborah's song to commemorate Barak's triumphal return from battle—" *Have they not divided the prey ; to every man a damsel or two.*"

But they will be sitting in their cosy rooms now. Some of them have concealed lighting, and most of them have very comfortable arm-chairs. Maybe they are thinking of me, and wondering why I could have been such a fool to have left them for this.

Christian is waiting for me on the delectable mountains, but he is so hemmed around with grace that even when he says he is undone, one gets the impression that he knows better. I am tired of Pilgrim and his mountain, and all the marvellous things he has to say, which shows, perhaps, there is something wrong with me. But he never had to deal with a woman pleading for liberty from a cruel husband.

I get up and peer into the street. It is deserted. A little smoke curls up from a few huts against the moonlight. I stroll quietly along the street and go into the church. This is the scene of the discipline cases. The darkness has erased it all. Two gigantic affairs in the lives of five people have vanished behind the backcloth of God's night.

The main door creaks, and I strain my eyes to see what it is. The door opens wide, and then closes, but I see no silhouette.

My blood begins to tingle. I think of Etienne Sokori and the little folk, and the spirits of the forest. There is a scraping, a slow methodical dragging. I sit back to await the result. Then, into the open between the front bench and the Communion table, comes a dark shape. It drags itself along until it is near enough to lift itself and cling to the wooden Communion rail. I cannot see well, but I know that this thing is human and I take a match from my pocket and strike it. There, praying to his heavenly Father, is a lad of twelve, paralysed from the waist down. I remember him well. One can see him any day lying in the road, or dragging himself along with slow painful intervals. He gets no physical help there at the rail. He is not cured and I do not suppose he will ever be cured. But if he can drag his broken body in faith to the rail, why should not I follow his example? It is easier for me to kneel there.

One's most obvious need is not necessarily one's greatest. This boy finds something here at the rail. I find, too, that I get nowhere, for all the kicking against the injustices of life, the ghastly cruelty of the bush and the ever-recurring suspicions and hypocrisies. Once again the broken body of man leads me to the broken heart of Christ, and I pray that, just as the five red roads reach out to these people, so His salvation may come to these villages, that others at home will be called to share with Him the " burden of the world's divine regret."

" O Jesus, Thou art our guide
And in Thy Life alone we have life:
Teach us to die that we may live.

By the shadow of Thy cross upon Thy cradle,
By Thine infant acceptance of the myrrh,
By the words that told of Thy decease upon
                                    the mountain top,
By Thy face set toward Jerusalem,
By Thy silence before Thine accusers,
By the joyful acceptance of the cross,
By the awful stillness of Thine incarnate life
                    uplifted before the world of men,
Pity our frailty.
Give us Thyself,
    that, nestling in Thy broken heart we may
    endure with Thee the agony of sinful man's
    return to holiness."

XIV

TWENTY-ONE babies have been baptised. Two have been turned away because their parents' membership was not in order. To those used to the European habit of christening, this is a most unchristian method of dealing with members. Poor old Rackstraw, when he saw children refused baptism, was aghast. " In my opinion that is absolutely contrary to the will of Christ," he said. " Would He turn away little children? I doubt it. I think the Mission is taking too much on itself in refusing to baptise children because of their parents' shortcomings."

But what Rackstraw could not understand is quite logical when examined. Children are baptised only when parents accept the vows on their behalf. Parents who are not Christians are neither capable of understanding, nor of carrying out, such vows. Parents, then, who cease to be members, are not given the chance to perjure their souls. Jesus, it is true, did not turn away the children;

neither do we. We look after them until they are old enough to make the vows themselves.

The service is now over, and the hurricane lamps have been brought out into the street. The choir is loath to break up, and snatches of hymns are taken up by the little groups assembled outside the church.

The sky is clear and lit by a thin moon. I decide to go to my lodging to get a little supper. The choir follows, determined to see me safely to my door. Why this anxiety to escort me, I wonder. We go slowly along the street. Coming to meet us is a solitary figure. I can see his legs plainly by the light of the lamp he is swinging. It is Gaston Techi.

" Hallo, Gaston. You were not in church tonight ? "

" Monsieur, you must come quickly; my wife has just given birth to twins."

" That's fine. What are they, girls, boys, or one of each ? "

" I don't know," he answers, " but please come; you must pray in our compound, for it is a serious thing to have twins."

Gaston speaks quickly and nervously to the choir members, and, as he talks and answers questions, we move on down the street. A general murmuring grows louder as we approach Gaston's compound, which, we find, is packed with people. A fire is burning in the middle of the compound and sending up a good deal of smoke. Beside the fire is a sack, and on it one of the twins. It is pink, and has a big head, and a withered little body. It looks uglier than it really is in this firelight. But I always contend that new-born babies have to learn to be beautiful, and it takes them roughly six months to master the lesson. They all succeed in the end, even those who remain ugly for the rest of their lives.

An old woman emerges from the black gap which is Gaston's street door. She looks very important, like an old hen who has become a foster mother. She has the second child, also stark naked, and she places it alongside the first.

The noise and the smoke worry me. I wonder what the mother thinks of it all. I expect she is so glad that all is over that fifty hollering people sound like a lullaby.

The twins look pinker as the fire gets brighter. They will look more wholesome when they are brown, the soft milk-chocolate brown of African babies.

It is extraordinary that these twins, because they happen to have come into the world in this part of Africa, will be left in peace. If they had been born in Dahomey there would have been palaver. In Twé, I met a local preacher and his wife who had recently had twins. The custom was that the wife should leave her husband until she gave birth to another child by another man. Luckily for all, the African minister's wife also had twins at the same time, and, as she refused to leave her husband to satisfy native custom, the local preacher was resolved to stand firm also. This saved a family catastrophe and a discipline case for the Church. But, when one of the twins belonging to the minister died, people wagged their fingers, and said: "We told you so. What else can you expect? They spurn the old customs and now they have to pay the price."

The fact that those who observe the tribal customs also pay, and very heavily, is often forgotten in a case like this. But the testimony is always present in the little images one sees in that part of Dahomey. They are sold in all the markets. These crude little figures in male and

67

female form are made especially to represent children. A woman will carry one in her cloth if she cannot take her child. All women with twins buy them, and carry one in front and one at the back. And, when children die, a little figure is set up in the house and is referred to as the one who has passed over.

Twins are a problem to many African tribes because, as one man said, " They are so unnatural." Fortunately for these little fellows on the sack, twins are looked on as normal in Bodou, though I wish things were a little cleaner. I remember seeing pictures of a maternity clinic in England. There were nurses holding up the babies behind plate-glass windows for their fathers' inspection. Those babies must have been as free of dust and dirt as the filament in an electric light bulb. If that is the reason for such close segregation they should live for ever. Embalming perhaps would be one step nearer complete preservation. But these little chaps on the sack are at the other end of the scale. They have already been bitten by dozens of malarial mosquitos, moths crawl over them at will, and only the crowd saves them from other larger insects and animals making a tour of inspection.

I shout my loudest to bring the din to an end. I pray for the happy family and, after the fervent " Amen " offered by everybody present, I pray silently for a woman evangelist, who can tell these proud mothers how to make the best of their children, to show them how, if there is only a sack for a cot, it can at least be clean. For, if Jesus had to make do with a manger, it was most certainly a clean one, else perhaps God's great plan of salvation through Christ would have miscarried in the first few hours of the incarnation.

XV

LEPRI has put down the mosquito net, but has forgotten to tuck it in. The last time he forgot, I had a tarantula as bed-companion. I walk round the bed with the hurricane lamp, looking carefully at all the folds in the net, and then I pull over the canvas chair to the wall and sit down. The day is over and black night is reigning, except where the new moon is putting down a weak white defiance.

Suddenly I become aware, as one becomes conscious of the ticking clock or the radio, of the noises of the African night, that incessant clicking and droning of millions of insects and animals. All the crickets, frogs, grasshoppers and beetles are out. Thousands of tiny luminous eyes are on the lookout for the enemy, while cries from as many mouths and legs betray their position. Away in the distance there are a dozen earsplitting shrieks of the bushbaby as he drags himself still higher up the tree. I pull off a sock, trying to remember the hymn I read this morning during my devotions and what I told myself about it. Somebody laughs outside and I get up and shut the door.

The noises of the night have again receded into the subconscious; there, yet not there, because superimposed on it all, in time with it, yet quite apart from it, there is the quick throb of the drums. What urgency! What incoherent speech and yet how full of meaning! I feel that odd tingling of the skin, the feeling I used to have as a child when a big dog came up to me and wanted to be friendly. I pull on the sock again and slip on my sandals. I open the door and step out into the night. There are several drums now and a noise like a ringing anvil. I go down the village with my lamp to see what is on. There are a few moving shadows in front of me, and I know I am going in the right direction. There is a light shining through the bamboo. They have bought three simple carbide lamps, and these give a cold white light to the clearing where some four hundred people are gathered.

The drums stop. Those who beat them are already hot, and wipe their faces on bits of rag. A young lad, standing with two small bars of iron, begins to tap out a rhythm. A drummer follows lazily with one stick. Then again that impatient staccato beat, and all the onlookers are galvanized into action.

The clearing has been well used, and now the dust begins to rise as men and women, dancing solo, move to the beat of the drums. The youth with the iron bars begins to sing. It is like the call of an animal to its mates. It is a couple of lines put to a scale altogether illogical to untrained Europeans like me. At the end of the two-line solo the whole assembly roars the repetition, and the dance has begun.

I can see the dust floating past the carbide flares and can feel it in my throat. It is impossible to analyse this dancing, yet it holds one. It fascinates and repels at the same time. A woman is moving slowly past me. Her feet are barely moving, but her hips and head are in strange revolt against the rest of her body. She has an expression of utter sadness, as though this dance represents what used to be, but now all, all is sorrow and death. She convulses, her feet move more quickly, her head goes forward oddly and her eyes open wide. There is frenzy in the world, and fear on her face. The sweat runs down from under her bandana on to her cheeks and shoulders.

The early missionaries forbade this dancing, saying it was immoral. They understood it better than I, perhaps, for to me it expresses nothing. There is nothing in my own experience with which I can compare it, or associate it. There are various movements one could call suggestive, but, whether they are or not, I cannot tell. The harmless movements are usually those which make the onlookers roar with laughter. Like the old man at Youhouli who came dancing before me, as stiff as a wooden soldier, save for an odd tremor of the head. As he came up close to me, he ducked and shot out sideways a trembling foot. The howls of laughter which greeted this embarrassed me, but inspired the old man to go on. Here was dancing of the old days, a dance which survived the scourge of the Prophet Harris. The tears of joy rolled down the faces of the people. Should I laugh with them, or should I be laughing at something which should be comdemned?

"What is he doing?" I asked a laughing bystander.

"He is talking to you," was the hysterical reply. "He says he is poor, and that he has not eaten all day, and would you give him some money. And when you do not answer, he says you are mean."

71

I took a twenty-five franc note from my pocket and tossed it to the old man, and the roar of cheers which greeted this was ample proof that my informant had given the right interpretation to the dance.

They are now going round in a circle, following one another in serried ranks and waddling like penguins. The drummers are glistening in the lamplight, and the sweat is gathering in the creases of their stomachs, and then trickling down. I walk away. Nobody cries out " Goodnight." They are all in their own world of crying crickets, croaking frogs and the dark forest.

I walk slowly back to the house. Even the barrier of culture is too high for man to scale. Only Christ can find a way through and make us one.

Before I get into bed I open the door wide. I have more fear of being stifled than being robbed. In all the journeys I have made, not once have I lost anything. Even pieces of string which are left behind are returned to Dabou within a few days. These people are honest.

I blow out the light and sleep.

I awake. It seems as if I have slept for not more than five minutes, but there is a cock crowing, and there is a chill in the air which calls out the dawn. A low, heavy thud, followed by deep rhythmic beating, tells me that somebody has died. I listen to this African dead march, this low, hollow vibration, almost mocking in its insistence. I wonder who is dead, and think of Augustin Gramel's second wife, the one who was expecting a child last night, the one I put under discipline. I wonder if she has died in childbirth, and if God is putting the same questions to her that I put to her husband. I turn on my back, and sigh and dose.

XVI

Years of experience of missionaries' needs have taught the suppliers to produce all kinds of gadgets. One of the most important is the canvas washbowl. I stand in front of mine now, and shave myself into reality. This is still Bodou, I think, and I have the Communion service to take before going on my way. The local preachers will be going to Dabou for their usual lesson on Saturday, and the class leaders' question-hour will take place the next time I visit the village.

A goat puts its head through the open door. Goats are impudent. The slightest encouragement and this one would be sitting at table eating my breakfast. Lepri chases it away as he comes in with the coffee he has prepared on a neighbour's fire. This is a French breakfast; bread, marmalade and coffee. Helen says coffee is not good for me, and that I drink it too much. But I am an addict, and would never dream of sending the pot away unless it was empty.

The church bell rings. The Protestants have their own method of ringing the bell; two quick strokes, and then a pause, repeated for about five or ten minutes. I know it is our bell. Within half an hour the service will begin. There are no stewards yet in these churches, nobody responsible for the bread and wine. The missionary brings it with him. Bread is rare in any case and is not seen unless somebody brings back a loaf from Dabou.

The church is nicely filled, the women on one side and the men on the other. I think, what a pity that in this, the most intimate of services, families are divided by sex. The men, too, are served first. To change this would create confusion, without bestowing an added right upon the women. They know there is only one order, and they do not feel insulted when they follow the men. Time alone will show them other ways. Much of what we consider bad form is merely unaccustomed action. Many of our missionaries are thought to be ill-bred because they never learn the lesson that one offers a seat to any visitor, however lowly.

Communion is important to these people. They will walk miles to attend a Communion service, or run back home from work if they hear the missionary has unexpectedly arrived in the village. On one occasion just after the war, when missionaries and African ministers were scarce, two ladies came to a village ten minutes after the Benediction had been given. With babies on their backs they had walked for five hours. They dropped to the floor by the side of the Communion table and wept.

These folk here now have come for something. Before me is a row of women. Their heads are held high and their eyes closed. All of them are mothers, some are very old with faces like carved king ebony, faces so sorrowful in repose that one is caught by the contagious sadness. All of them have that something in common, the haughty negro cheekbones giving the lie to the thick pursed lips, dry and cracked at this hour of the morning, as though they have struggled all night against an English east wind.

To these I give the wine and mutter: "Jezu dad nine: Na ell em etchi mebl," and I wonder what this symbolic blood means to them. They put their hands to their hearts as they rise to their feet and sway gently back to their seats.

Waiting at the door of the church is François Dabia. He says: "Give me medicine for this." He takes the cloth from his hand and shows me a dark wound surrounded by a green poultice. The hand is swollen and the fingers are shiny. Dirt, or perhaps the native medicine, has poisoned it.

"How did you do that?" I ask.

"Cut it with a matchet," he answers simply.

He follows me into the house and I get out my medicine box. It contains aspirins, cascara, quinine and dettol. The latter is the remedy. It is all I have in any case. I get a bottle and mix a little of the brown liquid with filtered water, and, as the colour changes to that of soapsuds, François realizes that he is getting something good—it even changes colour!

"Now," I tell him, " this will help you if you obey the instructions. There are lots of flies here and they want to

75

have their dinner just where your cut is, and if they drag their dirty feet all over it, then it will get worse. You have to keep those flies away, and this medicine will help you. Keep the wound moist all the time with this fluid, and it will get clean and heal up."

The poor fellow cannot thank me enough, and goes straight out to return with half a dozen eggs as a thank-offering.

I put back the medicine box. I cannot have anything more elaborate than that. But it is a terrible thought that I am perhaps the only man they see who can help them, except the "quacks,"—men with a little knowledge of medicine but with a great gift for making money. They do a great deal of harm. I do a very little good. What could I do, for example, for the young woman who sent for me at Sikensi? I entered her room. It was as black as night, and it took me a couple of minutes to get accustomed to the gloom. She sat in a corner with a very old lady, who kept up a desultory fanning with a home-made fly swatter. This poor girl had faded to a skeleton. One breast was nothing but a mass of putre-faction. Give her dettol? An aspirin? I gave her all I had of any value. I prayed. Then I came out and vomited.

When the lads came back from Dunkirk, burnt and torn to shreds, they came to a hospital where I was chaplain. The stretchers were three deep down the long corridor. I saw nurses crying. But everything possible was done for those brave fellows. One can ask no more. In the forest there are few doctors and nurses. More often than not there is only the missionary with his aspirins and dettol, followed by the booming of the death-drum.

I prayed for the girl at Sikensi. I know that prayer almost by heart now; I use it so often. It was the same prayer I used for the lad who had been bitten by a snake and who was being held in life, by two women, till death took him. His body convulsed at intervals, and his great white teeth bit on his muffled anguish. I arrived on the scene complete with aspirins and quinine, but it was the prayer of committal he received.

I go through the land with my simple medicine box. But how I long to do more! A nurse and a doctor could find here a great sphere of Christian service. Here one understands a little of the agony of compassion, and how Christ could not have endured without the gift of healing. What a prigilege to be qualified to take a real medicine chest to these people of the forest, to save lives, and then to let Christ save souls.

I tie the string of my bed-bag and Lepri carries out the chopbox to the van. In a few minutes my visit to Bodou will be over, and I shall be once again on God's red road trundling along toward the next village.

XVII

Two boys come racing towards the car as I press the starter. They want a lift, I suppose. They think I am returning at once to Dabou.

"Monsieur, Monsieur," they cry, as they come up breathlessly.

"You must wait; Monsieur Laurent is on the way."

"Monsieur Laurent?" I repeat.

"Yes, he is on the way back from trek."

Monsieur Laurent is the African minister in the Circuit. I can see him now, coming through a natural avenue of trees. He never hurries, but always arrives. He is wearing a grey shirt with shorts to match, and a light-coloured hat.

"What are you doing trespassing on my ground?" I ask teasingly.

" Ah, Monsieur," he answers, shaking hands, " I have just crossed the lagoon from Jackville and have come up this way to strike the main road for Toukpa."

" What is your news ? " I ask, in African fashion. His trek has taken him along the sea coast villages among the Alladian tribe.

" Everything is going well except that a prophet has appeared in the region of Adda."

" A follower of Harris ? "

" No, this one is filled with the spirit and prophesies and works miracles."

" Real miracles ? "

" Ah, monsieur, I am telling you what the people say."

The people believe they are real miracles. They take naturally to prophets. I remember the greatest of all the prophets I ever met. He was a Protestant turned prophet. He was Paul, the local preacher.

On the way back from a local preachers' class Paul fell in with a band of young men returning from the forest, where they had been to be healed of their wounds after a disembowelling ceremony. They were singing, and Paul joined in. He marched alongside a youth who carried in his hand what looked like crushed leaves. Whether the fact that Paul is a lusty singer decided what followed, is not clear, but just as his mouth was open at its widest, the youth popped in his handful of dried leaves. Paul spat, but his mouth felt as though it was burning, and the heat of it ran down into his chest. He was afraid, and ran on in front of the young men, and, getting into his compound, he cried to his wife to bring food and drink. It was in stretching for a morsel of goat-flesh that Paul became convinced that something serious had happened to him. His arm became locked in its outstretched position. Thoroughly frightened, he went to his room and threw himself on to his sleeping-mat. He slept. He saw a vision—a spirit who said: "Paul, Paul!"

"I am here, Lord," he answered.

"I am the Spirit of the river and you are my servant. To-morrow you must tell all the people in the village that I forbid them to eat goat meat. The goat is a filthy animal and is responsible for all the disease in the village and for all barren women."

Paul preached this not only in the streets but also in the church, and the people believed him wholeheartedly. Goats were slaughtered or sold until there was not one of their kind in the village.

Then the Spirit called again to Paul and told him to take a bowl of water into the street and to pray over it the Benediction. Paul lifted up his hands and cried: "In the name of the Father, the Son and the Holy Spirit." When he opened his eyes the water in the bowl was boiling.

"Paul," I said, as he got to this part of his story, "you are telling lies." But the people answered for him. They had been there. They had seen it with their own eyes.

"You have a devil, then, Paul," I concluded, and at once he confessed.

"I know I have a devil, and I want you to pray for me, that it may be driven out."

I prayed for him and he found relief at once. He cried out that he had been delivered of the evil spirit. He threw a twenty-five franc note on to the Communion table and strode out of the church praising God.

Within five minutes of leaving the church, Paul was in

a trance and crying and shouting blasphemy. He took with him nearly all the members of the Church, who were carried away by the wonders he performed. The steady work of twenty-five years fell like rotten fruit, to be trampled under foot by this pseudo-prophet. G—— is still trying to recover from that terrible relapse into paganism.

Now Monsieur Laurent has a similar problem. He will need all the help a praying Church can give, for he, more than the European, will be attacked and taunted. What has the Mission done for him that he is so faithful to it? He could be the owner of a great plantation, the richest man in his village, but he has renounced it, for what? To be a minister. And what is that after all? You can see he hasn't much by the way he goes about.

It is true; our African ministers are paid a minimum stipend which becomes altogether meaningless when one understands the significance of native hospitality. The few thousand francs paid to these hard-working men is swallowed in what we call Good Samaritan actions, in taking in the stranger as well as the friend, and feeding them.

This man is always tidy. He is naturally tidy. Others are unkept, and what they earn does not help them to be any better. There was one I saw taking prayers with that quiet dignity peculiar to the people of his tribe. His clothes were clean, but torn and patched. He thanked the Lord for his loving kindness, for food and clothes. To the cynic he was like the tattered banner of a defeated king. The pagan African would have the same impression. To him, a god is somebody who acts, but in a given way, as the Roman priest found when he went about destroying fetish shrines and groves.

" There," he said, " your gods are helpless; they do nothing to stop me."

When he returned home to his own village he found his church burnt to the ground. He was very angry and called on the Administrator, who had heard already what the priest had been doing. The chiefs of the neighbouring villages were called, but all agreed that surely the white man's God is capable of defending Himself. If not, then he is not worthy of worship.

Generally speaking, the African expects his fetish or image to be knocked on the head from time to time, but though they may not think it capable of looking after itself, they are quite sure it can look after its devotees. To see a minister in poverty, unable to take part in the common hospitality of the village, is a grave reflection on the minister's religion. Good training, adequate wages without entering into competition with commercial standards, and decent living conditions will go a long way towards saving the people in this country. To them it will be a practical application of the Gospel. They will not see, as some fear, good jobs with good pay, for all who become workers in the Mission, they will see only, God looking after His own.

" I will drop you down at the main road, then, monsieur."

" Where are you going now? "

" To Tisha."

He clambers in beside Lepri and we move off.

" *Au revoir*, Monsieur Laurent," cry the folk; " *Au revoir*, Ganga."

I reply to this last salutation with a wave, and the van glides out of the village. A Muslim trader approaches

82

with his loose limbs, his great bundle on his head. He walks miles to sell a piece of cloth, and he preaches wherever he goes. Already Islam has touched the coastal belt which was considered a Christian stronghold. The Laurents of this country will have to hold firm and help the people to keep faithful to their Lord.

The car turns slowly round the first hairpin bend, and, standing in the middle of the road, is a young African wearing only a loin cloth, and he is tearing off the lid of a sardine tin with his teeth! What a people! Strong, proud, independent and resourceful! The trouble is that, just as this youth makes do if he hasn't a tin-opener, so he may make do if he is not supplied with a genuine faith in the God and Father of our Lord Jesus Christ.

XVIII

I SET down Monsieur Laurent at the main road where it crosses the private road of the oil-plantation. He waves farewell, and I watch him go slowly down the slope towards Toukpa.

Before me is the great red road, one of the five red gashes serving this district. It runs on straight for half a mile and then disappears into that black gap which is the forest. It is like the wounded hand of Christ reaching down into the valley of the shadow of death. I race toward that black spot as though I expect to see the hand withdrawn with somebody saved for life eternal.

QUESTIONS FOR THE ROAD

Chapter I

1. Europeans teach the value of every second. Africans ask: "Why waste time on trivialities?" In England we complain if folk come late to church. What about Africans?
   (a) Are they to be excused because of age-old customs?
   (b) How can one decide what is the result of slackness and what the result of custom?
   (c) Are they right and we wrong?

Chapter II

2. "Time makes ancient good uncouth." Can we say the same for righteousness?

3. If a tribe is a thousand years behind the times, must its conception of righteousness be also primitive?

4. How would you distinguish the sinners from the saints in such a tribe?

Chapter III

5. When Samuel Nomel pays his hundred francs to a hospital worker he is no better than the non-Christian.
   (a) Has he the right to accommodate Christian ideals to existing conditions or even to deny these?
   (b) Is a paid Christian worker of this type a hindrance to the progress of Christ's kingdom in Africa?

Chapter IV

6. Should a missionary call concern the family, or should a man decide for himself and, in some cases, for his dependents?

7. What would you do if your partner were called overseas and you were not?

8. If an unsympathetic person can retard the work of the Church, should not the Missionary Society in its own interests, quite apart from its divine mission, take steps to guide, if not control, the marriages of its workers?

Chapter V

9. Etienne Sokori believes in spirits and the little folk. Would you say that this disqualifies him from being a Local Preacher?

10. Tribal rules have the group, rather than the individual in mind. Are we wasting our time seeking individual conversions within the tribes? Would a more general presentation of the Gospel to the people as a tribe or clan produce better results? How could this be done?

Chapter VI

11. "Meet the non-Christians on their own ground," we are told. Others tell us to take the best from local religion and Christianize it.

(a) How shall we know what is best?

(b) Could fear, as the African knows it, be used to bring him nearer to God?

(c) What are your comments on Keble's lines taken from his hymn: "When God of old came down from heaven . . ."?

"Come, Lord; come, Wisdom, Love and Power;
Open our ears to hear;
Let us not miss the accepted hour;
Save, Lord, by love *or fear*."?

Chapter VII

12. Why have Church schools, if it is known in advance that the Government intends to take over all education?

13. What is the difference between Christian education and religious instruction?

CHAPTER VIII

14. What would you think if you found yourself in church sitting next to a man with leprosy?

15. If there are no colonies near enough to allow a leprosy patient to go away from his village, should he be denied the right of Christian worship and fellowship?

16. Of course, you do not believe in magic, but how would you deal with a person who does? For example, how would you treat the Local Preacher who drank the fetish potion?

CHAPTER IX

17. Is it essential to reduce to writing the language of every tribe so that all may read the Word of God in their mother tongue?

18. If you believe that small tribes must learn another language to become literate, would you suggest a European language because of its breadth, or an African language because of its appeal through similar thought-forms?

CHAPTER XI

19. What do you know about Laubach?

20. If a person shows a sincere desire to be saved from his sins, yet cannot pass the entrance examination for membership in the Church, should he be refused admission?

CHAPTER XII

21. What is the Biblical evidence against polygamy?

22. Is there any argument for polygamy?

23. Why is polygamy such a problem in Africa?

24. The following are two generally accepted beliefs:

(a) Economic conditions will eventually kill polygamy:

(b) A less severe attitude toward polygamy would make Christianity more popular.

Since the end of polygamy is a foregone conclusion, why not take this step toward the conversion of Africa by opening the Church to polygamists?

25. If people have not made vows before God, is their marriage just as binding?

Chapter XIV

26. If you were sent to open up a new mission field, what would be your attitude to converts' requests to have their children baptised?

Would your answer be based on:
(a) The Bible?
(b) History?
(c) Expediency?

Chapter XV

27. There are some African dances which are said to be immoral. Should all dances be prohibited by the Mission on the argument of " the weaker brother "?

Chapter XVI

28. "I wonder what this symbolic blood means to them." Does that really matter?

29. It has been suggested that all missionaries have some medical training. Others argue that a little knowledge can do great harm. What do you think?

Chapter XVII

30. To employ all the African ministers we need to meet present opportunities, we should have to pay very low stipends. Should the opportunities before us decide our policy, or should we think first of the needs of the individual and pay a reasonable stipend to a few?

NOTES ON "QUESTIONS FOR THE ROAD"
by The Rev. A. W. Banks, M.A., B.Sc.

The Organisation of African Society (see Question 3)

African society usually has a complicated structure with detailed customary laws regulating relationships between persons in the tribe and stating clearly what things are permitted and what are not permitted. The whole social structure is closely related to religious beliefs and practices which provide sanctions governing the people's actions. Family and sex relationships, inheritance, the use of property, service for the community, labour, government and all other activities of the tribal group are controlled by this customary law.

Would you dare to use the word "primitive" in describing this social and legal structure? Are its practices and ideals "a hundred years behind the times" remembering what has happened in the world in the twentieth century?

Gifts and Bribes (see Question 5)

There are customary gifts which must be given by a man when he approaches a person in authority in most African tribes. By this the person's authority is recognized. It was often one of the legitimate ways by which in the past a chief, for instance, obtained any remuneration. Is this satisfactory? Consider these payments in relation to the inadequate salaries often paid, particularly to minor officials.

When considering how widespread bribery and corruption appear to be in modern African Society, consider also the position in countries in Europe and America; consider methods used by some for gaining positions of authority; consider the system of tips, of giving favours, drinks, meals, etc. in the hope of getting some special consideration in return.

Note the concern being felt by Africans in certain areas (e.g. Gold Coast and Nigeria) about bribery and corruption in Government and trade. At the end of 1953 a Northern Nigerian report, drawn up by an almost entirely African Committee, has recommended the radical reform of the customary gifts system and the use of "legislation and education as the main means to this end." They recommend the abolition of certain customary gifts, e.g. "any gift in connection with a court case, any gift from a daily labourer to his headman, any gift to a superior which customarily he would have to return more generously." They list permissible gifts, which are those sanctioned by obligations of public life, by charity and by hospitality. They recommend an extensive publicity campaign and proper salaries for minor officials.

Consider the responsibility of the corporate Christian fellowship in regard to this problem and to methods being suggested for its solution. Consider then the Christian individual's responsibility in the situation, both as a member and as a paid worker of the Church.

BELIEF IN SPIRITS (*see Question* 9)

In Africa such beliefs as those of Eitienne Sokori are held not only by illiterate and uneducated (in the Western sense) but by many educated people. Some well educated Christian Africans say "I know that my education and my reason tell me that little folk do not exist but I have seen them." What do they mean? These are genuine, thoughtful, intelligent people. Are they, because they are in the puzzling transition stage of tension between the old and the new thought, thereby disqualified from preaching the Christian Gospel?

Similar beliefs were held in Europe in the not very distant past and compare the present day superstitions of many rural peoples. Are Europeans clear about the powers of evil in the world? What about discussions regarding a personal devil? Are European Christians delivered from all fears of evil?

Study again the New Testament stories of spirits and of Jesus' healing of demon-possessed people. Is there a message here for those who believe in spirits to-day? How should it be presented so that Jesus is known to be a real Saviour in the fullest sense of the word?

GROUP CONVERSION (*see Question* 10)

Europeans are so used to presenting the Christian Gospel as the offer of God to the individual, and are so sure that it is necessary to get an individual decision if salvation is to be real, that the idea of the conversion of a clan or a tribe is considered to be impossible. Study the problem carefully and objectively.

Group responses were made to the preaching of such men as Prophet Harris (the Ivory Coast) and Samson Opon (Ashanti). If possible consult a detailed examination of Indian mass movements. (See G. E. Phillips: *The Untouchables' Quest*, 1936; J. W. Pickett:

Christian Mass Movements in India, 1933). An individual is strongly controlled by the group in African society and group conversion has often taken place. An individual's decision is frequently the stimulus that leads to the response of the group. When a group, family or clan, enters the Christian Church together, the individual is not torn away from his social group. There is the danger that the decision is not a deeply spiritual one, though this by no means follows. There is the risk that old customs will survive in the group and that the old moral level will be kept. Consider, however, the difficulties met with when individual decision alone is insisted upon and converts are taken out of their old grouping.

After-care is essential if group conversion is allowed. There must be regular and continuous instruction and regular and frequent worship must be provided. Where this happens notable social progress follows. Schools are needed for the education of the children. Pastoral care must be constant and thorough. The health and the social and economic welfare of the communities must be sought. One approach is that, where an individual from a family or clan makes the decision to become a Christian, he be asked to postpone his baptism until most or all of his kinship group are also ready for baptism.

The Church and Education (*see Questions 12 and 13*)

In West African education the churches have led the way. governments have followed. The vast expansion in Sierra Leone, Gold Coast and Nigeria has, until recent years, been almost entirely the work of the churches, with Government finance. Should Church or Government cater for rapidly extending educational needs of modern West Africa?

The Church can continue to set standards in Teacher Training, contribute to Government policy, develop special branches of education, e.g., Agricultural Colleges, Blind Schools.

What makes education distinctively Christian?

Leprosy (*see Questions 14–15*)

See *Who Walk Alone* (author on staff of B.E.L.R.A.) for a vivid story of a leper's sense of loneliness and the contrasting life of usefulness in a leper community. See also *Leprosy and Methodism* and *African Angelus* " I am a leper."

Translation (*see Question 17*)

There are about 700 languages spoken in Africa, some (like

Yoruba) spoken by several hundred thousands, others confined to small tribes perhaps 10,000 strong. How can books be printed for such a small number? What is the alternative?

There are advantages in using the language of a larger African group: it belongs to the same racial group, it is spoken by other Africans, it may have similar thought forms.

There are also advantages in using French or English. They are more fitted for expressing the ideas of the modern world, books are already available, and they admit a person to new literature and a new culture, making them citizens of the world.

Dr. Laubach (*see Question* 19)

Dr. Laubach was a missionary from America to people in the Philippine Islands. He found that they had no written language.

He worked out a scheme for teaching adults to learn to read the language they spoke in a very short time. He has taught his method to people in many countries of the world. It has been used in parts of West Africa. Thousands of adults there have learned to read in a fortnight or less. (For the story of his work see *The Silent Billion Speaks* or *Nothing Can Stop it Now* by F. C. Laubach). The method consists of finding the simplest way of making the association between the idea expressed in a word that is spoken and the same word written down. The person does not have to learn the language —it is his mother tongue. The motto of the campaign is " each one teach one." In a dozen lessons many illiterates can learn to read. Laubach sees a great opportunity of evangelism in this literacy movement (see also filmstrip " A World of New Readers "). Note the great need for suitable books for those who have newly learned to read. How are they to be provided?

Polygamy (*see Questions* 21–25)

The Old Testament includes records of polygamy amongst the Hebrews. Discover the process by which polygamy gave place to monogamy in Old Testament times. The New Testament assumes monogamy. Why?

Seek to discover what the Bible indicates to be God's intention in marriage. Look up the following passages: Genesis ii. 24 and Mark x. 7–8; Exodus xx. 14; Deuteronomy v. 18; Matthew v. 27–28; Hosea ii. 19–20; Ephesians v. 25, 29, 32. (What view of marriage is implied here by St. Paul?) Examine the New Testament meaning of love. What does this imply for marriage?

(See also *The Bible and Polygamy*—Parrinder.)

Arguments advanced in Africa for polygamy include: there are more women than men and therefore polygamy is the only way of ensuring marriage for all; if there is more than one wife then the work of the house and the farm is shared and more produce can be grown; polygamy produces more children in the family than monogamy; to have more than one wife gives added prestige to a man; women prefer polygamy. Each of these statements needs examination: not all are true. (Study, for instance, H. C. Trowell: *The Passing of Polygamy*.)

Polygamy has been the custom in many African societies for centuries. The arguments mentioned above have great force for the African. The fundamental problems are economic and social. The whole family system is involved. Monogamy seems so hard. It is often not understood.

Economic conditions have, in the past, tended to the passing of polygamy. They will probably have much the same effect in Africa. At the same time many wealthy Africans desire to have more than one wife because they can afford to have them, and they consider it gives added prestige. The family system is being affected by economic changes.

There are constantly repeated demands for polygamy to be allowed in the Church. Many of the separatist sects in Africa have allowed polygamy and have often separated on this issue. Note the request on these lines made by the African representatives at the Tambaram Conference of the International Missionary Council in 1938. It was the representatives of the other Younger Churches who said that such a procedure was unthinkable. Monogamy has to be shown to be a way of marriage which is not specifically that of the white man, but is accepted by people of many races, and is essentially a Christian way.

Can the sanctions of religious marriage, a vow before God, be applied to the civil marriage, a contract between partners? What should the Church do about civil marriage under native customary law?

The Church needs to find a way of maintaining its standards of marriage while showing every sympathy and offering all the power of God's grace to those who find monogamy hard or who fail in their attempts to carry it out.

TRIBAL DANCES (*see Question* 27)

It is often true that African Christians, particularly the older ones, are more critical of African dancing than are Europeans. They are most unwilling to allow Christians to be involved in any way in African dancing.

At the same time dancing, rhythmic movement is in the very blood of most African people. Women taking part in a Christian procession of witness will do so most naturally with a dancing rhythmical step. Is it not possible to get intelligent African Christians, both educated and uneducated, to consider African dancing in all its forms and to give some guidance to younger Africans on the subject? In most churches in Africa the commands about dancing must come from African Christians themselves rather than from Europeans.

MEDICAL AID (*see Question* 29)

Anyone with open eyes and a sensitive heart who travelled in West Africa, would pray for hospitals and dispensaries and would wish he were a doctor. The need is unbelievably great and the number of skilled persons able to deal with it alarmingly small. A few simple drugs wisely handled could alleviate much suffering. Co-operation between Government and Church in medical service has only developed comparatively recently. Plans are being made for a United Christian Training Hospital in Nigeria, helped by Government funds. But so very much more needs to be done at the highest level, for all the people and not only for a few.

* * * *

In trying to answer all these questions think in terms of the Church which God has raised up in Africa. The members and leaders of that Church—and they are Africans—are the people who, with the missionaries, have to answer these questions every day. To desire to answer the questions should involve, at the same time, praying for those whose life and conduct depends on their discovering the answers.

Printed in England by Lawrence Bros. Ltd., London and Weston-super-Mare (4875)